Debt

Money and Me

Debt

by
Christina J. Moose

Rourke Publications, Inc.
Vero Beach, FL 32964

For Elliott and Ontheway,
who will manage well

———————

Photo on page 2 by Jim Whitmer.

Produced by Salem Press, Inc.

∞ The paper used in these volumes conforms to the American National Standard for Permanence of Paper for Printed Library Materials, Z39.48-1984.

Library of Congress Cataloging-in-Publication Data
Moose, Christina J., 1952-
    Debt / by Christina J. Moose.
        p.   cm. — (Money and me)
    Includes bibliographical references and index.
    Summary: Introduces debt, credit cards, bankruptcy, and related money matters.
    ISBN 0-86625-610-5
    1. Consumer credit—Juvenile literature. 2. Debt—Juvenile literature.
3. Consumer credit—United States—Juvenile literature. 4. Debt—United States—Juvenile literature. 5. Children—Finance, Personal—Juvenile literature. 1. Children—Finance, Personal—Juvenile literature. [1. Credit cards. 2. Debt. 3. Finance, Personal.] I. Title. II. Series.
HG3755.M57   1997
332.7—dc21   97-10254
                                                                              CIP
                                                                              AC

First Printing

PRINTED IN THE UNITED STATES OF AMERICA

Contents

Chapter 1   Good Borrowing, Bad Borrowing 6

Chapter 2   Are You Creditworthy? 11

Chapter 3   Loans and Lenders 17

Chapter 4   Shopping for Deals on Debt 24

Chapter 5   Revolving Debt: The Credit Card Merry-Go-Round . . 30

Chapter 6   In Over Your Head: Dangerous Debt 38

Glossary 44

Sources 46

Index 48

Good Borrowing,
Bad Borrowing

Neither a borrower nor a lender be,
For loan oft loses both itself and friend.

A father said these words to his son in a play written by William Shakespeare more than four hundred years ago. The father is warning his son that it's not a good idea to borrow money. Borrowed money is always hard to pay back, and the friend who lends it to you usually gets angry if you don't pay it back on time. Result? You lose a friend, *and* you still have to pay back the money. If you have ever lent even a few dollars to someone who forgot to give it back, you probably know what Shakespeare means.

These days, people still borrow. In fact, it's hard to get through life without borrowing—and not all borrowing is bad. Some reasons for borrowing are good ones, like buying a house. Other reasons for borrowing can get you in trouble.

This book is all about borrowing: good borrowing, and good ways of doing it—and the trap of bad borrowing, and how to escape it!

Loans and Debts

Another term for borrowing is "taking out a loan." A *loan* is something of value that somebody lets you use. A person or organization that gives you a loan is called a *lender*. Most lenders ask you for something in return for letting you borrow, but not always.

Many businesses give free loans every day. Utility companies, for example, let your family use water, gas, electricity, and telephone services. Your parents don't have to pay for these things until *after* you have taken a bath or phoned your best friend. Doctors and dentists provide medical services, but they don't send the bill for their work until *after* you have your check-up or get your teeth cleaned. These services are not money loans, but you still get something of value before you pay for it.

Usually, though, people think of borrowing money, not services, when they think of taking out a loan. Such borrowing is also called *debt* (pronounced DEHT), and the borrower is called a debtor. A debt is like a loan, but it is not quite the same. Most of the time, a debt is the loan amount *plus* an additional amount that you pay the lender for letting you use his money.

Save some of your allowance in a piggy bank or "rainy day jar" in case of an emergency.
(James L. Shaffer)

"Wants" are not a good thing to buy with borrowed money. (James L. Shaffer)

Grown-ups worry a lot about this creature called debt. It sounds bad, and often it is bad, especially when it grows big. It's only dangerous, though, when you don't understand how it works and let it get out of control. If you learn how to tame it, a little debt can help you get through emergencies or buy things that you will need and use for a long time.

Why Borrow?

People borrow when they do not have enough money to get things they either *need* or *want*. There is a big difference between these two types of borrowing.

Borrowing for wants is always a *choice*—a decision you can make but one you do not have to make. For example, in the story called "Borrowing for 'Wants': Jake and Mando," Jake wants a chocolate dessert. He thinks about borrowing money from Mando, but he

---

BORROWING FOR "WANTS": JAKE AND MANDO

Jake was nearing the head of the lunch line when he saw the dish of chocolate pudding sitting on ice in the dessert section. It cost fifty c]ents — fifty cents that he didn't have that day. He thought about whether to skip the dessert or to ask his friend Mando, next to him in line, to lend him two quarters.

Jake looked at Mando's tray and noticed that he had no pudding either. Mando loved chocolate pudding, so maybe he didn't have fifty cents either. Jake also remembered that he would not get his allowance for another week. "Better skip it," Jake said to himself.

remembers that he won't be able to repay Mando for a week. Jake *decides* not to borrow — to "skip it."

Borrowing for needs is different. Read "Borrowing for 'Needs': Beth and Olivia." Emergencies like Beth's sometimes leave people with no choice. Beth has to get home. She cannot "skip" that! Beth is a good planner, though. She has saved some of her allowance in her Rainy-Day Jar and repays her *creditor*, Olivia, right away.

Both Jake and Beth know something about "good" borrowing: They know when to borrow, and when not to borrow. They also care enough about their friends to think about how borrowing might affect them.

Why Not Borrow?

Some people hear that question and think, "I only live for today. *Why not* spend all my money, and then borrow so I can buy things I want right now?" Other people, like Beth and Jake, hear the same question and think, "Is this thing *really* important to me? Can I repay what I must borrow in order to buy it?"

What did you think?

There are many reasons *not* to borrow. It's not very smart to borrow money for something you don't really need, like a CD, unless you know you can pay it back soon. It's also not smart to borrow if the lender asks you for something that is more valuable to you. For example, it's sort of stupid to promise your older brother that you'll wash his truck for two months, or give him next

---

BORROWING FOR "NEEDS": BETH AND OLIVIA

Beth and Olivia were almost at the bus stop when Beth noticed the hole in the pocket of her backpack. After feeling for her wallet, Beth realized it was gone. She panicked for a moment, then told her friend what had happened and asked to borrow a dollar for the bus ride home. Olivia was happy to lend her the dollar. When Beth got home, she took a dollar from her Rainy-Day Jar.

Then she and her Mom got in the car and returned to the school to look for the wallet. When it turned dark, they had to give up, but on the way home they stopped at Olivia's house. Beth paid her the dollar she owed. "You could have waited until tomorrow," Olivia said, but Beth told her friend she liked to pay her debts right away, before she forgot.

GOOD DEBTS, BAD DEBTS

Don't Borrow for These Things (Save up instead!)
- Things that cost a lot (more than $100) *but* you don't need: stereo, CD player, roller blades
- Things that cost less than $100: CDs, video games
- Things that you will use up before you would finish paying for them: movies, fast food, sports tickets

It's Okay to Borrow for These Things:
- Emergencies: doctor's bills, emergency transportation, car repairs, airplane ticket to see a sick family member
- Things that cost a lot (more than $100) *and* that you will use for a long time: a computer, a car, a house

---

week's paper-route money, if he'll lend you money for one little soda. Finally, it's not even honest to "borrow" money if you know you won't be able to pay it back. That's pretty much the same thing as stealing.

Believe it or not, some grown-ups borrow money for such reasons. As a matter of fact, when it comes to debt, some grown-ups can be pretty stupid. Why? Because they have many more ways to borrow than kids have. These adult ways of going into debt are very easy to start, but very hard to control. You'll learn about some of them in this book. If you pay attention, you may end up smarter than these grown-ups!

Buying a computer on credit can be a good reason to borrow, because you will use the computer for a long time. (Ben Klaffke)

CHAPTER 2

Are You Creditworthy?

Young people usually don't have to borrow, except in emergencies. Then they can go to their parents for help, or maybe a friend. When Olivia gave Beth a dollar for the bus, she already knew two things:

- Beth *needed* the money.
- Beth was trustworthy; she would repay the dollar soon.

Parents, and friends like Olivia, have known you for a long time. They know whether you can be trusted to repay a loan. When you grow up, though, those who lend you money will not always be family and friends.

A Word About Trust: Credit

Many institutions lend money to adults: banks, department stores, credit unions, finance companies, and others. These lenders usually don't trust you at first. After all, they don't know you. You can't just promise Cool Rags Clothing that you will pay next month for the sweater you want today! Lenders first have to find out how trustworthy, or *creditworthy*, you are. In fact, the word "credit" comes from an old Latin word meaning "trust."

When you grow up, lenders determine your creditworthiness by looking at three things: your *work history*, which shows how responsible you are; your *income*, or how much money you make; and your *credit history*, or how well you have repaid past debts. After high school or college, you will get a job. You will begin building a work history and earning an income. However, you will not have a credit history until you have borrowed some money and paid it back on time.

That presents a problem: How can you get a loan without a credit history? Yet how can you get a credit history without getting a loan?

Establishing Good Credit

One way to establish good credit is to begin early—right now, in fact. You can open a *bank account*, such as a checking account or a savings account, long before your turn eighteen. Some banks will let you open an account with as little as $25. Your parents will have to go with you to the bank when you *deposit* (put in) and *withdraw* (take out) money. Then the bank will keep track of how

---

ARE YOU A GOOD "CREDIT RISK"?
WHAT LENDERS LOOK FOR

- **Income and assets:** How much money do you earn at your job? That's your *income*—and the more, the better. If you are applying for a very big loan, such as a mortgage to buy a home, the lender will probably also look at your *assets*, or *capital*: the value of all the big things you own, like a car, stocks, and other property.
- **Job history:** How long have you worked at your job? The longer, the better. Your employer probably thinks you are a good worker and will let you keep your job. The lender will think that you are a responsible adult and will honor your promise to repay your debts.
- **Credit history:** How good a borrower have you been in the past? Have you paid your bills on time, or are you always late? Have you ever failed to repay a loan? You have? You lose! Even if your income and job history look great, you need a good credit history to get a loan.

Before you can build a good credit history, you need to open a bank account and learn to manage your money wisely. **(Ben Klaffke)**

you handle your account. Do you make regular deposits? Do you try to withdraw more than you have?

If you learn how to handle your account responsibly, your bank may allow you to apply for a major credit card, like a MasterCard or Visa, when you turn eighteen. Your parents could simply add your name to their own credit card,

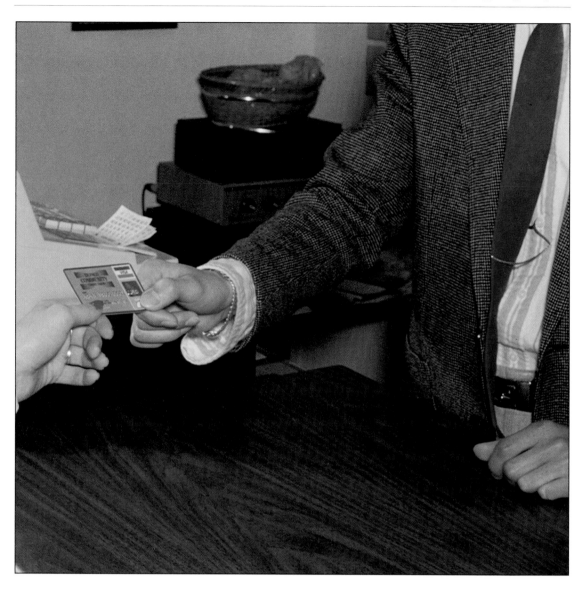

You can apply for a credit card after you turn eighteen.
(James L. Shaffer)

but that will not help you establish a credit history. To do that, you must have your own credit card — with *your* name on the card's account as the person who will pay the bills. You must then use this card to buy something.

It should be something you need and will use for a long time, perhaps a computer. Buying things this way is called "buying on credit" or "buying on time." You have been given a loan. The store will allow you to take home the computer before you are able to pay for it. You, in turn, promise to make monthly payments until the loan is repaid.

You are now officially *in debt*, and you will pay a price for buying things this way. The cost of the loan, called *interest*, will be figured as a portion, or percentage, of the cost of the computer. That percentage is called the *rate*. For example, if the computer costs $1,000, and you take one year to pay for it at a rate of 18 percent, you will pay $180 just for the interest: $1,000 × 0.18 = $180. When you add the interest to the computer's original cost (called the *principal*), the total comes to $1,180.

Notice that, if you had saved your money and paid cash for the computer, it would have cost only $1,000. Because you bought the computer on credit, it cost $1,180. Actually, you bought two things: a computer for $1,000, and a loan for $180. It costs money to borrow money!

CREDIT BUREAUS: THE "BIG THREE"

Credit bureaus keep records on the credit histories of nearly everyone in the United States. If a lender denies you or your parents credit, or if you think that someone has reported wrong information, you should contact these agencies and they will give you a copy of your credit history. If you just want to see a copy of your credit history, you can get one for a small fee. The three largest credit bureaus are listed below.

Equifax Credit Information Services
P.O. Box 740241
Atlanta, GA 30374-0241
(800) 685-1111

Trans Union Corporation
555 West Adams
Chicago, IL 60661
(800) 916-8800

Experian
(formerly TRW Information Services)
P.O. Box 8030
Layton, UT 84041-8030
(800) 422-4879

As you make your payments for the computer, you are establishing your credit history. Agencies called *credit bureaus* keep credit histories for everyone who borrows money. Their records show who lent you the money, how much you owe, and whether you were late in making your payments. If you were so late that a bill collector had to remind you to pay, that will also appear in your credit history.

All sorts of lenders, from banks to car dealerships, go to credit bureaus whenever they want to know the creditworthiness of someone applying for a loan. If they see that you borrowed money to buy a computer but your payments were late or you missed some payments, you probably won't get the loan. If they see that you made your payments every month, they will know that you are a responsible person who repays debts. You will probably get the loan.

Loans and Lenders

If you think about it, anyone who gives you a loan is taking a risk. What if you *default*? In other words, what if you fail to repay the money? Basically, a lender has two ways of lowering this "credit risk":

(1) by asking you to give up something valuable until you can repay the loan, *or*

(2) by charging a high price (interest) for the loan.

Secured Loans

A *secured loan* provides the lender with something of value in case the borrower defaults. This thing of value is called *collateral*. For example, Jake might offer to let Mando hold on to his calculator if Mando will lend him fifty cents for chocolate pudding. When Jake repays Mando, Mando returns the calculator. If Jake defaults on the loan, then Mando gets to keep the calculator.

Loans for very expensive items—like cars, boats, business equipment, and diamond rings—are almost always secured loans. If you live in a house that your parents bought, they probably had to take out a secured loan called a *mortgage*. A mortgage is probably the biggest loan you will ever need in

People who need a loan often go to a bank. (James L. Shaffer)

your lifetime, because a house costs a lot of money, even more than a car. It takes about three to five years to pay for a car, but it takes most people thirty years to pay for a house. That's why the word "mortgage" comes from Latin words meaning "a promise until death"!

How is this loan secured? First, when you buy a house you pay a large sum of money, called a *down payment*. This "down" is thousands of dollars, but it's still only part of the cost of the house. You get the rest of the money as a loan from the bank or some other lender.

Next, the house itself is the collateral. If you cannot make your monthly mortgage payments, the lender can take the house and sell it. This sounds scary, but most lenders make sure that you can pay before they will approve the mortgage loan. How? By checking your work history, your income, and your credit history. So don't worry—if your parents bought your house, the lender is pretty sure they are able to pay for it.

Unsecured Loans

An *unsecured loan* requires no collateral. Sometimes this type of loan is called *unsecured credit* or simply *credit*. You usually need an excellent credit history before you can get such a loan. Lenders take a greater risk in making this type of loan, so they want to feel very sure that you can, and will, repay your debts.

These days, though, some lenders will give unsecured credit to people whose credit histories are not that good. At first that doesn't seem very smart—after all, the lender is taking a big risk. However, the lender makes up for this risk by charging a very high rate of interest. Some lenders issue credit cards with rates as high as 20 percent. That's more than twice the rate for most home loans! These lenders of unsecured credit—especially issuers of credit cards—make so much money from the interest that they are willing to take a bad risk now and then.

Because credit card debt is such a problem in our society, a whole chapter of this book (Chapter 5) is devoted to it. The thing to remember about unsecured credit is this: *You will always pay a higher price for an unsecured loan.*

Money, Money: Who's Got the Money?

People who need to borrow money can go to different types of lenders, depending on why they want to borrow the money and how they want to pay for it.

$$ *Banks and Thrift Institutions.* You may already have a checking or savings account at your parents' bank, or at a "thrift" institution like a savings and loan association (S&L). Banks and S&Ls can arrange loans for most expensive items, including car loans and home loans (mortgages). Some banks specialize in making loans to businesses. Some offer *home equity loans*, secured loans that use your house as collateral and have special tax advantages. Nearly all of these institutions issue major credit cards, like MasterCard and Visa.

Because banks and S&Ls are in business to make a profit, they charge competitive interest rates, depending on the type of loan and whether it is secured or unsecured. Their rates for unsecured credit can be pretty high. However, their rates for secured loans, like mortgages, can be very reasonable. They are careful to make sure you can pay, so it will take a while for them to do the paperwork, called *processing the loan*. If you are not a good credit risk, you may not get your loan. If you have a good credit history, though, an S&L or a bank can be a good place to get a loan.

$$ *Credit Unions.* People who have something in common can form credit unions. Such groups may be teachers or people who all work for the same company. They may be people who are in the military or people who belong to a particular church.

Credit unions are in business to get the best deals for their members, not to make a profit.

A loan officer will discuss the loan with you and ask you about your credit history. (James L. Shaffer)

Because they are *nonprofit organizations*, their loans usually cost less. Also, their loans can often be approved and funded in a shorter period of time. That means the borrower can get the money faster.

People use credit unions to buy things like furniture and appliances, but credit unions also offer mortgages and credit cards. To find out if there is a credit union that you or your parents can join, you can call the Credit Union National Association at (800) 356-9655.

$$ *Finance Companies.* These companies are in business *mainly* to make loans to people. They lend money for *second mortgages*, when people need more than one loan to buy a house. They also arrange *installment loans*, to buy things like furniture, a washing machine, a television, a computer, or a car. Installment loans help people pay for such things within a specified period of time, like five years, in monthly payments.

Finance companies tend to charge high rates of interest for these loans. That's because they will loan to people who have poor credit histories. Such people often would not be able to afford some of the things they need without being able to pay monthly. However, the borrower ends up paying lots of money in interest—sometimes even more than the original cost of the item.

If you are interested in arranging an installment loan, you should compare the rates offered by the bank and the store where you are buying the item. One of these places might give you a better deal.

$$ *Retail and Other Businesses.* Many stores and companies carry their own accounts and will arrange installment loans (discussed above) or issue their own credit cards, sometimes called *charge cards*. Department stores, furniture stores, computer stores, oil companies, and even airlines will issue charge cards so you can buy their

Finance companies are in business to make money by lending money. (James L. Shaffer)

products and pay later. Sometimes you can establish a credit history with one of these stores and then get a major bankcard, like MasterCard or Visa, at a lower rate.

♥ *Family and Friends.* When you are young, borrowing from parents, brothers and sisters, or even a friend is okay now and then—if you pay the money back right away. Young adults sometimes borrow the down payment for their first home from parents.

Still, it's usually better to avoid borrowing from friends and family. Not all parents can afford to keep helping their children after they reach adulthood. Also, if you fail to pay back a loan, the lenders—the most important people in your life—might feel hurt or even angry.

If you do borrow from friends or family, you must be businesslike. Agree on a fair rate of interest and set dates for monthly payments. Write everything down so there are no misunderstandings. Above all, make your payments on time. You could lose more than your good credit history!

☹ *Bad and Dangerous Lenders.* There are many other places to borrow money, but you should stay away from some of them. *Pawnshops* will give you a cash loan if you leave a valuable thing, like jewelry or a camera, at the shop. However, the cash is only a *very small* portion of the item's value. If you fail to repay the loan on time (usually only a few days or weeks), the pawnshop will sell your treasured item to the first person who comes along.

Even worse, criminals called *loan sharks* will be happy to lend you money for interest rates that are so high you would have a very hard time repaying the loan. This crime is called *usury.* Such criminals are dangerous and might hurt you, or those you love, if you do not pay your debt on time. Better to stick to banks, credit unions, and honest retailers!

CHAPTER 4

Shopping for Deals on Debt

When you need a pair of sneakers, do you buy the Air Pair that costs $135, or do you buy the shoes on sale for $50? Shopping for a loan is like shopping for anything else: You've got to be a bargain hunter to get the best deal!

Most lenders are in the business of making a profit by selling loans. The more you pay in interest, the more money they make. The cost and terms of a loan will vary depending on where you get it, whether it is secured or unsecured, and how much risk the lender must take.

Compare Prices and Terms

In 1968, the U.S. Congress passed a law called the Consumer Credit Protection Act. This law says that lenders must honor Truth in Lending: They must provide certain information to borrowers. This information makes it easier to compare the costs of several loans. Two pieces of information are especially important: the finance charge and the annual percentage rate (APR).

Finance Charge. The finance charge is the *cost of the loan in dollars*. It includes how many dollars

Shopping for a good loan is like shopping for any other bargain. Ask about details, and beware of bargains that sound too good to be true! (James L. Shaffer)

you will spend on interest, and how many dollars you must spend on additional fees to process the loan. These fees depend on the type of loan or credit. Home loans, for example, charge fees for checking your credit history and appraising the property's worth, among other things. Credit cards have late fees (extra charges if you don't make your payment on time) and sometimes annual fees. The total of all the interest plus all the fees is the finance charge.

Annual Percentage Rate (APR). This is another way of understanding the loan's cost. This time, the cost is shown as an *annual percentage of the amount you want to borrow.* The APR does not include other fees, like late fees and annual fees. The higher the APR, the more the loan will cost when you are all done repaying your debt. You want a loan with a low APR.

Let's say you want to buy a car. That's probably a long way off, but even if you don't have your driver's license yet, it's not that hard to understand.

The car you have chosen costs $12,000, and you will give the dealer $2,000 as a down payment (a partial payment that tells the seller you are serious). Now you need a loan of $10,000 to drive away in that car.

Car loans are secured loans (see Chapter 3): If you default, the lender can always seize your collateral, the car. Therefore, interest rates for car loans are not as high as they are for unsecured credit. The table "Shopping for a $10,000 Car Loan"

TRUTH IN LENDING

The Consumer Credit Protection Act of 1968 requires lenders to provide the following information so that people who need a loan can compare the costs of different loans:

- **Name** of the company providing the loan or credit
- **Annual Percentage Rate (APR):** the cost of the loan as a percentage of interest across one year
- **Finance charge:** the cost of the loan in dollars, including all interest and other charges and fees, *and* how these are calculated
- **Schedule of payments:** how much you must pay (or the minimum due) and how often (monthly? weekly?)
- **What is included in payments:** principal, interest, taxes, etc.
- **Grace period** (important for credit cards): how long until the lender starts charging interest
- **Other fees,** including annual fees and late fees

SHOPPING FOR A $10,000 CAR LOAN					
Lender	APR	Finance Charge	Monthly Payment	Years	Total Debt
Al's Auto Loans	8.25%	$1,329	$318	3	$11,329
Bank of Yourtown	8.25%	$1,783	$249	4	$11,783
Car Loans for Less	8.5 %	$2,323	$209	5	$12,323

shows you some of the choices you might have. The choice you make will depend on what is most important to you.

Do you want the lowest monthly payment? Then you might choose Car Loans for Less. This lender gives you the longest period of time to pay off the loan, five years, and a monthly payment of only $209. However, Car Loans for Less charges the *most*: It has the highest interest rate (APR), and you will also pay this rate for a longer period of time. This loan is therefore the most expensive, with the highest finance charge.

If the total cost of the loan is most important to you, you would be best off with Al's Auto Loans. The cost of this loan will be nearly $1,000 cheaper, although the monthly payment is high. Al wants his money fast, so he's willing to let you have his loan for a good price—*if* you pay him more every month.

If you cannot afford Al's $318 per month, but you still want to keep the loan's cost as low as you can, Bank of Yourtown might be best for you. This bank probably knows that lots of people are in your shoes: They don't want to spend thousands of dollars in interest, yet they don't have enough for Al's high monthly payment.

Interest Rates: Fixed or Adjustable?

Some lenders have another way of "playing with numbers" to get the best price for their loans: They can charge interest either at a fixed rate or at an adjustable rate (also called a variable rate). As if there weren't enough things to consider when you are loan-shopping, here's a new twist!

For a *fixed-rate loan*, the interest charge is computed at the same interest rate for the entire period of the loan. If you agree to pay a fixed rate of 8 percent, that is the rate at which the interest will be calculated until your debt is repaid.

An *adjustable* or *variable rate* does just that: It adjusts, or varies, over the time you are paying the loan. The rate can go up or down, according to an *index* (another interest rate recognized as a standard).

Why would anyone want to buy a loan whose interest cost is uncertain? That depends on whether you think the index rate will go up or down. When rates are going up, the price of an adjustable-rate loan will increase, too. When rates are going down, the price of the loan also falls. If you believe that future interest rates will stay the same or fall, then an adjustable rate might be right for you. If you believe that rates are going up, you might want to "lock in" a fixed rate of interest at today's lower rate.

The choice between an adjustable-rate and a fixed-rate loan is most important when you buy a house and go shopping for a *mortgage*, or home loan. If you decide on a fixed-rate loan, and if rates are rising, you will pay less for the loan in the long run. If rates are dropping, you should pick an adjustable rate.

Of course, lenders look at it the opposite way: When interest rates are dropping, they like to sell fixed-rate loans. That way they can "lock in" today's higher rate of interest before it drops tomorrow. When interest rates are rising, lenders like to offer adjustable-rate loans. Sometimes they even offer a a very low "teaser" rate—at first. Then, in a few months, the rate suddenly "adjusts" upward, and the lender gets richer from the higher rate you now must pay.

Buyer Beware!

Finance charges, annual percentage rates, adjustable rates, fixed rates—these are just some of the things you will need to think about when you shop for a loan one day. Right now, the main thing to remember is this: *Lenders are in business to make a profit from your need to borrow.* They might offer you a "deal on debt," but the deal is usually best for them.

If you must go into debt, limit your borrowing for the big things that you really need, not luxuries you can do without. Then shop for the "debt deal" that gives you the interest rate and payment period that suit you best.

Revolving Debt: The Credit Card Merry-Go-Round

In the last chapter you learned something about car loans, home loans (mortgages), and installment loans. These are examples of *closed-end credit*: You borrow money to purchase a specific thing, and repay that loan over a specific period of time, such as four years or thirty. At the end of this period, you have repaid your debt and the lender "retires" the loan.

Most credit cards, on the other hand, offer *open-end credit*, or *revolving credit*. In other words, you can use a credit card to purchase all sorts of different things, not just one. You can also pay for these things as quickly or as slowly as you like. As long as you pay a *minimum payment* each month, you can put off repaying your debt.

This sounds like a great "debt deal" except for one thing: The interest you pay for this type of loan is high—sometimes 19 or 20 percent. That's a lot when you consider that interest for most other loans is around 7 to 9 percent! Still, many people have credit cards because they are very easy to use.

Types of Credit Cards

There are two types of credit cards:

- **Major cards:** These cards, like Visa and MasterCard, are usually issued by financial institutions like banks and credit unions. You can use major credit cards to buy things from many different stores and businesses.

Truth in Lending laws require the lender to tell you the annual percentage rate (APR), the grace period, and any extra fees. This lender advertised an APR of only 3 percent, but notice how it jumps to 13.9 percent after a short time.
(James L. Shaffer)

- **Retailer cards:** These cards are issued by *retailers*: businesses that sell things to the public, like department stores, oil companies, or furniture dealers. You use this type of card to buy only what that business sells.

How to Get a Card

Like any other lender, issuers of credit cards need to know that you can and will pay your bills. You must therefore prove that you are creditworthy before you can get a credit card. (Go back to Chapter 2 to find out how to build a good credit history.)

You usually cannot get a credit card before you turn eighteen. Then, if you get a job, you will need to keep that job and make some money for a year or so before a bank will let you apply for a credit card.

A few credit cards, called *secured credit cards* or sometimes *debit cards*, are not really credit cards at all, but they are a good way to build credit when you are young and just starting out. These special cards require that you deposit money with the lender before you can use the card. Then you can purchase items up to the amount you deposited. You might ask your bank whether it issues debit cards.

If you are eighteen and in college, some banks have a special plan: They will issue a "student card" even if you have no credit history. Student cards limit your purchases to a total of only $300 to $500. This amount is called your *credit limit*. If you pay your bills on time, your credit limit can grow, giving you more buying power.

Before you even think about getting a card, though, you need to know how revolving credit works. While you're waiting to turn eighteen, this might be a good time—because in the world of credit cards, what you don't know *can* hurt you.

WHO'S GOT THE BEST CARD?
WHAT TO LOOK FOR

- *Interest* will be charged if you do not pay the full amount of the bill every month. The amount may be reasonable or very high, depending on the rate of interest and how the lender calculates it. Look for a rate under 14 percent.
- *Grace Period:* Does the lender charge interest from the moment you buy something? Or do you have at least 25 days to pay your bill before interest will be charged? Look for a 25-day grace period.
- *Annual Fee:* Some lenders charge you just for letting you use their card. This fee has nothing to do with your purchases—you will pay it whether you use the card or not. Look for a card with no annual fee.
- *Other Fees:* How much does the "late fee" cost you if your payment does not arrive on time? Are you charged a "transaction fee" each time you make a purchase? Look for a card that does not have transaction fees.

How Does It Work?

When you use a credit card, your lender will send you a bill for your purchases, usually once a month. The bill will show your *transactions*: what you bought, where you bought it, and how much each item cost. The bill will also list a *minimum payment*—only a small part of the total that you owe. You can pay just this minimum, but watch out.

Remember that using a credit card is the same as getting a loan. If you pay just the minimum, the lender will charge interest on the remaining part of this loan, called the *new balance*, or simply *balance*. The bill will show other charges, too, including late fees and sometimes annual fees. Most lenders will allow you a *grace period*—a certain number of days until the time they begin to charge interest—but some will not.

Lenders who issue credit cards are happy to give you a card and let you pay the minimum every month. Why? If you pay only the minimum, they can charge interest on your balance and make lots of money. If you pay the full balance every month, the lender won't make much.

Yourtown MajorCredit Card

Account #1234 56XX8
Credit limit: $2,000.00
Available credit: $975.00

Send payment to:
Bank of Yourtown
555 Creditworthy Way
Yourtown, CA 90000

Questions?
Lost or stolen cards?
Write to us, or call:
800-555-0000

Statement closing date: 12/20/97

Previous balance:	$ 500.00
Payments (Thank you):	– 350.00
Purchases and debits:	850.00
Finance charges:	10.37
New balance:	**$1010.37**
* **Minimum payment due:**	**$50.52**
Payment due date:	**1/14/98**

Transactions

Date	Transaction #	Description	Amount
11/21	78311O2XK9RRR	Computer City	$105.00
11/27	99235AB23NT2X	College Way Bookstore	75.00
12/03	444DF6X88312K	Seafood Heaven	50.00
12/04	78311ZZ9XX23S	Santa's Toy Barn	45.00
12/07	7345NP2WYA344	Music Mania	25.00
12/15	3422ERT8Y877T	Cool Rags Clothing	150.00
12/18	30999XP45R1YM	Payment — Thank you	– 350.00
12/20	1Y2DDP344DED7	Kate's Roadside Repairs	400.00

Finance Charges

Days in Billing Period	30
Average Daily Balance	$691.17
Finance Charges	$10.37

Annual Percentage Rates (APR)

	Monthly Periodic Rate	APR	Average Daily Balance
Purchases	1.50%	18%	$ 691.17
Cash Advances	1.50%	18%	$ 0.00

* Notes to Our Customers:
You may pay the minimum payment due. If you pay less than the New
Balance, your next bill will include additional finance charges.
Keep paying the minimum! We like charging you interest! Happy holidays!

The Minimum Payment Monster

Let's say you're now in college. You get some income from a part-time job, and some from your parents. You have a major credit card, and you use it for clothes, books, computer supplies, and other things you need. The card is easy to use and safer than carrying lots of cash. Besides, you pay off your full balance every month or two, so you are not going deeply into debt.

Then you begin to buy more things with your card: You take your girlfriend to dinner for her birthday. You look really cool putting your card on the tray when the waiter brings the check. The holidays are coming up too, so you use your card to buy some gifts. On your way home for vacation, something unexpected happens: Your car breaks down, and the mechanic tells you it will cost $400 to fix. Who has $400 in cash? Thank goodness for your credit card!

By the time you get your next bill, you're $1,000 in debt. It's a little shocking how quickly it's built up! Then you see the "minimum payment due": Your lender will allow you pay just $50.52 this month. Thank goodness for the minimum payment!

But watch out: The lender also charges interest at an annual percentage rate (APR) of 18 percent. Your minimum payment is about to become a monster. If you pay *only* the minimum every month, it will take you nearly five years to pay off this loan—*if* you stop buying things with your card. When you are all done, you will have paid almost $500 in interest. That's a lot for a $1,000 loan!

How to Be Credit-Smart

The very best way to escape the "minimum payment monster" is to pay your full balance every month—or, at most, over two months. If your bill is still too big for you to pay, you are spending more money than you have. That will make you a slave to debt, because you will have to spend your *future* income paying for your *past* expenses.

Here are a few other tips for handling your credit cards wisely:

It's not a good idea to have too many credit cards. If you use them all at once, you could get into dangerous debt.
(James L. Shaffer)

- *First, look for the the lowest interest rate and fees.* Decide on a card based on your personality and habits. Do you pay your bill in full every month? Get a card with no annual fee. Do you need to pay over two or three months? Get the lowest interest rate, even if there is a small annual fee.

- *Second, stick with <u>one</u> major credit card.* As you get older, many lenders will want you to use their credit cards, especially if you have a good credit history. Don't be tempted to apply for lots of different cards. The more cards you have, the easier it is to use them and get into debt.

- *Third, don't use your card for luxuries.* CDs and going out to dinner are luxuries. Use your card for needs, like school supplies, and emergencies, like doctor visits and car repairs.

Credit cards are not "plastic money," as some people seem to think. Remember: You'll always get the best credit deal from *yourself.* In other words, if you save your money first, and buy afterwards, the cost of your "loan" will be absolutely free!

In Over Your Head: Dangerous Debt

The point of this book has been to tell you about borrowing and to show you ways of avoiding bad debt when you grow up. Still, what if something unexpected happens? What if a tree falls on your house or you break your leg and cannot work? What if you simply forget to keep track of your spending and buy too many things? Adults can make mistakes, just like children. However, adults cannot ask Mommy or Daddy to pay their debts.

Use Your Savings

If you have money in a savings account, you should use it to pay your creditors. When the loan's interest charge is higher than the interest you earn by saving, it is far better to pay off the debt than to save the money. Why? Because you will lose more money paying high rates of interest than you will gain by saving.

Let's say you owe your creditor $10, and she charges 8 percent every month until you repay that debt. If you let a month go by before you pay off your debt, you will owe $10 *plus* $ .80, or $10.80. If you let another month go by and the lender

compounds your interest payments, you will owe interest of 8 percent on $10.80—an additional 86 cents. Wait two months, then, and you owe a grand total of $11.66. You paid $1.66 for your ten-dollar loan.

Let's also say that, during this whole time, you had $10 in a savings account that earned 4 percent interest. You thought, "I won't withdraw my savings to pay the lender, because I want to keep my savings and earn the interest." How much did you earn? In two months, compound interest plus your savings of $10 came to only $10.82. You earned 82 cents in two months.

That sounds good at first, but remember: While you were earning 82 cents, you also increased your debt by $1.66. Your "savings" actually *cost* you 84 cents ($1.66 - $ .82). It would have been smarter to withdraw your $10 and repay your debt right away, before even one month went by.

Get Help Fast

If you have no savings and you cannot repay a debt, *contact the lender*. Lenders won't let you forget your debt, but they also don't want to lose your business. Often they will help you find a way to repay your debt over time.

What if you cannot pay many bills—not just one? What if you are so late with some of your payments that bill collectors are calling you? That's more serious. Again, you should contact the lenders to try to work out a way you can pay them. However, you'll need more help than that.

Several support groups are listed at the end of this book. One source of help is the National Foundation for Consumer Credit. This organization has offices across the United States called Consumer Credit Counseling Services. A CCCS counselor will help you establish a way to manage your debt. You can call (800) 388-CCCS to find the office nearest to where you live.

Bankruptcy: A *Last* Resort

The very last resort is to file *bankruptcy*. Filing bankruptcy is both hard and expensive to do. You must go through the courts and pay a lawyer to help you. Also, you must give nearly all your property—including most of the value of your home and car — to the court. The court then sells your things to help pay your creditors.

Going bankrupt is not an "easy way out," as some people think. Your credit history will show the bankruptcy, and you will be unable to get credit for many years. In addition, the stress of going bankrupt can ruin a person's life. You are always better off if you can avoid filing for bankruptcy — even if you have to sell your possessions and ask your family for help.

Examine Your Feelings

Of course, you are not in debt now. One day, when you buy a car and a home, you will go into debt — *good debt*, for good things.

If you have read this book with the help of a parent or a teacher, you already have some ideas for staying out of *dangerous debt* when you get older. There are also things you can do right now — before you ever get your first loan or use

The biggest loan you ever get will be for your home—an example of a good reason to go into debt. (Jim Whitmer)

your first credit card — to avoid dangerous debt. The most important one is this: *Talk with your parents about feelings and money.*

Sometimes feelings rule the way we act. When it comes to spending, that can get you into lots of trouble. Even grown-ups allow advertising to make them think they "must have" things they really don't need for a happy life. TV commercials, home shopping networks, and the advertisers on the Internet want you to buy, buy, buy! Everyone seems to tell you, "If you buy my makeup you will look beautiful" or "If you buy my four-wheel truck you'll be healthy and athletic."

The message is: "*Things* can make you happy." The truth is, things don't always make you happy. In fact, when you buy too many things and get into dangerous debt, that can make you very, very unhappy.

It is important to know something else: Advertisers who sell things and the lenders who issue credit cards do not care if you are happy. They only want you to spend your money in this

---

THINGS YOU CAN DO TO AVOID DANGEROUS DEBT *NOW*

- Talk to your parents about money, your allowance, and how to spend it.

- Decide what you *really want*: You can't have everything, but you *can* save for things that are really important to you.

- Try saving a few dollars from your allowance each week for about ten weeks. Use a jar like Beth's Rainy-Day Jar in Chapter 1. Then take *half* of the money out of the jar and treat yourself to something you really want. (Save the other half for emergencies.)

- Build a spending plan, or *budget*, to keep track of how much money you have and how you are spending it.

- Find ways to cut costs: Take a sandwich and an apple to school for lunch, and stay away from expensive sodas and fast food.

- Find ways to earn money: Offer to mow the neighbors' lawn or take care of their cat when they go on vacation.

WAYS TO AVOID DANGEROUS DEBT WHEN YOU GROW UP

- When you get your paycheck, pay your bills *first*, and in full, before you spend on luxuries.

- Pay *yourself* next: Set aside some money, no matter how small, for savings. This money should be placed in a separate account that you do not touch unless an emergency arises.

- Learn about *insurance* to avoid big emergency expenses. You can start by calling the National Insurance Consumer Helpline at (800) 942-4242.

- *List* the things you *need* to buy before you go shopping, and do not buy anything unless it is on your list.

- If you have more than one credit card, choose *one* major card with the lowest interest rate. Cut up the rest and mail them back to the cards' issuers.

emotional, *impulsive* way. They would like you to *think* that their things can make you happy, so you'll buy them and they can get rich. It's a trap, and lots of people fall for it.

Don't let someone else tell you what you want. Decide for yourself! When you do, you'll avoid the trap of dangerous debt.

Glossary

annual percentage rate (APR): the cost of a loan as an annual percentage of interest.

balance: amount owed on a credit card or other loan.

bankruptcy: a legal procedure for paying debts with the help of the court.

closed-end credit: a loan of a specific amount of money to purchase a specific thing, to be repaid in a specific amount of time.

collateral: something of value you promise to give a lender in case you cannot repay a loan.

credit: a loan based on trust that you will repay.

credit bureau: an agency that keeps credit histories for people who borrow money.

credit card: a plastic card issued by a bank (bankcard) or other lender that allows you to purchase items and pay for them later. Sometimes called a *charge card*.

credit history: a record of how you have repaid past debts.

credit limit: the total amount you are allowed to spend using a credit card.

credit union: an organization that works to get the best deals for its members.

creditor: someone to whom you owe money.

creditworthiness: the likelihood that you will repay a debt; trustworthiness.

debit card *or* secured card: a card used to buy things up to an amount you have deposited in a bank account.

debt: money that must be repaid; the amount you owe a lender for a loan, including principal and interest.

default: to fail to repay a debt.

finance charge: the total cost of a loan in dollars.

finance company: a company whose main business is to make a profit by lending money.

fixed-rate interest loan: a loan whose interest charge is computed at the same rate for the entire loan period.

grace period: the number of days until you are charged interest for a credit card loan.

impulsive spending: spending based on feelings.

income: the total money that "comes in" to you, including allowance, earnings, and gifts.

installment loan: a loan to buy an expensive item in periodic payments over a fixed number of months or years.

interest: the cost of borrowing money as a percentage of the principal.

loan: something of value, usually money, that a *lender* lets you use, usually for a price.

minimum payment: the least amount that must be paid on the balance of a loan.

open-end credit: revolving credit.

principal: the original amount of a loan, not including interest and fees.

rate: a percentage of interest.

revolving credit: a loan that allows you to carry a balance forward.

secured loan: a loan that provides the lender with something of value in case the borrower defaults.

unsecured loan: a loan that requires no collateral but instead is based on creditworthiness.

Sources

Books

Berg, Adriane G., and Arthur Berg Bochner. *The Totally Awesome Money Book for Kids and Their Parents*. New York: Newmarket Press, 1993.

Berry, Joy. *Every Kid's Guide to Intelligent Spending*. Chicago: Children's Press, 1988.

Blue, Ron, and Judy Blue. *Money Matters for Parents and Their Kids*. Nashville, Tenn.: Thomas Nelson, 1988.

Drew, Bonny. *Moneyskills*. Hawthorne, N.J.: Career Press, 1992.

Godfrey, Neale S., and Carolina Edwards. *Money Doesn't Grow on Trees: A Parent's Guide to Raising Financially Responsible Children*. New York: Simon & Schuster, 1994.

Otfinoski, Steve. *The Kid's Guide to Money: Earning It, Saving It, Spending It, Growing It, Sharing It*. New York: Scholastic Inc., 1996.

Organizations and Support Groups

Bankcard Holders of America
524 Branch Drive
Salem, VA 24153

Keeps records on credit cards with lowest rates and fees. Also publishes educational brochures on the wise use of credit, including "Establishing Credit for the First Time" and "Getting Out of Debt."

CardTrak
P.O. Box 1700
Frederick, MD 21702
(800) 344-7714

Sells a listing of the best credit card deals (lowest rates and fees) for a small fee.

Credit Union National Association

P.O. Box 431
Madison, WI 53701
(800) 356-9655

Call the toll-free number to learn if you are eligible to join a credit union.

Debtors Anonymous

General Service Board
P.O. Box 400
Grand Central Station
New York, NY 10163-0400

Helps people who repeatedly get into debt to examine and change their behavior. Write to this organization for a list of meetings in your area.

Family Service America

11700 W. Lake Park Dr.
Park Place, Milwaukee, WI 53224
(800) 221-2681

Supports family life though education, including credit and debt counseling.

National Center for Financial Education

P.O. Box 34070
San Diego, CA 92163
Web site: http://www.ncfe.org

Helps card holders who need to learn how to manage credit, including information aimed at children and young adults.

National Foundation for Consumer Credit

8611 2nd Ave., Suite 100
Silver Spring, MD 20910
(800) 338-CCCS
Web site: http://www.nfcc.org

Supports Consumer Credit Counseling Services, with offices across the United States. Counselors educate consumers in the wise use of credit and help those in debt to set up plans to pay creditors.

Index

Adjustable-rate loan 28
Advertising 42
Annual fees 33, 36
Annual Percentage Rate
 (APR) 26, 44

Balance 33, 44
Bank account 12
Bankruptcy 40, 44
Banks 19
Bill collectors 40
Borrowing 6

Car loans 26
Charge cards 21
Closed-end credit 30, 44
Collateral 17, 44
Consumer Credit
 Counseling Services
 40, 47
Consumer Credit
 Protection Act 24, 26
Credit 19, 41, 44
Credit bureaus 15, 44
Credit card debt 19,
 35-36
Credit cards 13, 19-20,
 25, 30-33, 35-37, 44
Credit history 12, 15, 18,
 22, 32, 44
Credit limit 32, 44
Credit risk 17
Credit Union National
 Association 21, 47
Credit unions 20, 44
Creditor 9, 44

Creditworthiness 12, 32,
 44

Dangerous debt 38-43
Debit cards 32, 44
Debt (defined) 7, 44
Default 17, 44
Deposit 12
Down payment 18, 23

Family and friends 11, 22
Feelings and money 42
Finance charge 24, 26, 44
Finance companies 21,
 44
Fixed-rate loans 28, 45

Grace period 26, 33, 45

Home equity loans 20

Impulsive spending 43,
 45
Income 12, 45
Index 28
Installment loans 21, 45
Interest 14, 19-21, 23,
 26-27, 33, 36, 38, 45

Job history 12

Late fees 33
Lenders 7, 16, 29, 40, 42
Loan 7, 45
Loan sharks 23

Major credit cards 31
MasterCard 31

Minimum payment
 33-35, 45
Mortgage 17-18, 28

National Foundation for
 Consumer Credit 40,
 47
National Insurance
 Consumer Helpline
 43

Open-end credit 30, 45

Pawnshops 23
Principal 15, 45

Rate 45
Retailer cards 32
Revolving credit 30, 45

Savings 38, 40
Savings and loan
 associations (S&Ls) 19
Secured credit cards 32,
 44
Secured loans 17, 26, 45
Student card 32

Thrift institutions 19
Transaction fee 33
Transactions 33
Truth in Lending 24, 26

Unsecured loan 19, 45
Usury 23

Variable-rate loan 28
Visa 31

Withdraw 12